Original title:

Herbal Harmonies

Copyright © 2025 Creative Arts Management OÜ
All rights reserved.

Author: Giselle Montgomery
ISBN HARDBACK: 978-1-80566-629-5
ISBN PAPERBACK: 978-1-80566-914-2

Elysian Echoes

In the garden where peasants pot,
Grew a carrot who fancied a lot,
He dreamt he could dance,
In a twirly romance.

The radish exclaimed with a cheer,
"Your moves, dear friend, are quite queer!"
The turnip just laughed,
At the veg-dancing craft.

In a stew pot, the veggies would play,
Mixing tunes in their watery bay,
A basil played bass,
While oregano gave chase.

Then came a pearl onion surprise,
Whose tears flooded all with their cries,
"Stop the madness, I plead!
Can't handle this speed!"

But the beets just rolled right on by,
With a jig, and a prance, oh my!
In the sun's golden beam,
They all danced, it would seem!

Strumming with the Stem

In the garden, plants do play,
With leafy guitars, they strum all day.
The basil sings in a jazzy tune,
While thyme taps toes to the light of the moon.

Cilantro shakes its frilly hair,
As mint and sage dance without a care.
The rosemary croons, so soothing and sweet,
While carrots keep rhythm with their tap dancing feet.

Rhapsody of Resilience

A dandelion in the corner, looking bold,
In a suit of sunshine, never growing old.
It winks at the weeds, with a chuckle or two,
'Try keeping up, I'm not done with you!'

The sturdy oaks play a symphony grand,
While the shy lilacs lend a fragrant hand.
With laughter that rustles through petals and bark,
Nature's own choir sings bright in the park.

Tantalizing Tinctures

In a pot, the herbs take a swirl,
With a pinch of garlic, and watch them twirl.
Sage flips pancakes and giggles with zest,
While parsley says, 'I'm simply the best!'

Fennel throws parties with a licorice flair,
While chives add a wink, saying, 'Life's a fair!'
Their blends make a potion, a magical brew,
That tickles the tongue, and makes you say, 'Ooh!'

Verse of the Valley

In the valley of green, the critters conspire,
To brew up a mischief, with laughter and fire.
With badger as maestro, and fox as the star,
They dance with the daisies, giggling afar.

The sunflowers wave in a comedic show,
As rabbits recite lines in a chorus of 'Whoa!'
With clover as backdrop, a stage ever bright,
The valley's a laugh, from morning 'til night.

Whispers of Wild Leaves

In the garden, a basil waltz,
Tomatoes giggle, the thyme exalts.
Parsley whispers, 'Oh, come dance!'
And mint jokes, 'I'm the best at romance!'

Chives wear hats, looking quite grand,
While spinach tries to take a stand.
Cilantro swaggers with a grin,
Saying, 'I'm the spice that makes you spin!'

Echoes from the Garden

Carrots' laughter in rows so neat,
Radishes hiding with nimble feet.
A cabbage sighs, 'This weather's odd,'
While broccoli's standing; a vegetable god!

Peas in pods have a sneaky plan,
To start a band called 'The Veggie Clan.'
With lettuce leaves clapping in cheer,
They sing of dressing that brings everyone near!

The Essence of Earth and Moon

Under the stars, the herbs convene,
Sage tells tales, quirky and keen.
Rosemary giggles, 'I'm hard to forget,'
While lavender sighs, 'I'm the best at reset!'

Dill dances roots, making quite a scene,
While fennel whispers, 'Life's a cuisine!'
Chervil with friends, spices take flight,
Sparking joy like a firefly's light.

Symphony of Scented Brews

Tea leaves gather, a jam session bold,
Peppermint raps, 'I'm never too old!'
Chamomile's beat drops, relaxed and sweet,
While oolong swings to a funky beat.

Lemon balm chimes in, a zestful cheer,
Sipping laughter, adding good cheer.
With honey coaxing, a buzz is found,
A melody made, in cups we drown!

The Alchemy of Fragrance

In a pot where mint dreams of pie,
Basil takes a dive, oh my,
Coriander sings a silly tune,
Thyme sways lightly, under the moon.

Fennel prances like a fool,
Oregano sits by the pool,
Garlic giggles, a pungent cheer,
While rosemary plays peek-a-boo near.

Sage shares jokes from ancient scrolls,
Peppermint spins in fragrant shoals,
Cilantro dances with such flair,
Each herb in a role, so debonair.

In this garden, joy does bloom,
With laughter trailing in their plume,
Potions bubbling with quirky plans,
When nature's green makes merry bands.

Melodies in the Meadow

Daisies hum their sunny spree,
While clovers offer lemonade for free,
Buttercups sway with a giggling breeze,
And violets whisper secrets to the trees.

Tall grass joins in, tickling toes,
As dandelions burst with laughter that grows,
A bumblebee buzzes a funky beat,
In the meadow, the rhythm is really neat.

Ladybugs shuffle on the warm ground,
Beetles tap dance all around,
With each bloom dressed in laughter's grace,
Nature's concert brings a smile to the face.

Fragrant aromas glide high in the air,
Breezes carry tunes beyond compare,
The meadow sings a symphony sweet,
Each petal and leaf makes the music complete.

The Quiet Dance of Flora

At dawn, the tulips start their jig,
While daisies wiggle, oh so big,
Snapdragons open with a grin,
As morning dew begins to spin.

Chrysanthemums join in with zest,
Each leaf rehearsing for the best,
While ferns gracefully kick and sway,
Wishing for flowers' big debut day.

Even the mushrooms join the game,
Shrooming and booming, seeking fame,
In this garden, every shade,
Finds a partner in a leafy parade.

With petals flapping like silly fish,
And roots tapping to a secret wish,
A quiet dance that brings delight,
In nature's realm from day to night.

Infusions of Serenity

Chamomile whispers a sleepy song,
While lavender hums along,
Mint leaves frolic with a splash,
Creating brews that make hearts dash.

Ginger adds spice with a little grin,
While honey stirs in, ready to win,
Lemon peel twirls, oh what a sight,
In this cauldron, flavors ignite.

Each sip a giggle, a charming tease,
Rose petals swaying in the sweet breeze,
Tea bags gossip, they know the score,
Of cozy cups that leave us wanting more.

In a teapot's warmth, we find our cheer,
With herbal hugs that draw us near,
Infusions bubbling with laughter bright,
Turning each moment into pure delight.

Soundtrack of the Seasons

In spring, the daisies dance with glee,
Bees buzz tunes, both wild and free.
The grass sprouts high, a leafy crowd,
Nature's band plays loud and proud.

Summer brings a sizzling song,
Lizards groove, they can't go wrong.
Watermelons hum, bright and sweet,
A carnival of fruits to eat.

Autumn's leaves start to sway,
Crisp crunches mark the fading day.
Pumpkin pies serenade the chill,
Each flavor adds a joyful thrill.

Winter's chill wraps snug and tight,
Frosty sounds crackle in the night.
Hot cocoa's warmth, a soothing rhyme,
It's snowman giggles, every time.

Tones from the Tinctures

A dash of mint and a twist of zest,
In a bottle, spices jive, they jest.
Ginger leaps with a fiery kick,
While chamomile's soft, a calm little trick.

Orange peels spin in merry waltz,
Their zest adds cheer, no faults or faults.
Lavender whispers soothing tunes,
While rosehips croon to the lazy moons.

Basil jazzes up a pasta dish,
With a pesto dance, who could resist?
Cinnamon swirls, oh what a song!
With every sip, the taste feels strong.

From tinctures brewed in sunshine's glare,
Comes laughter, joy, and fragrant air.
Each little drop, a vibrant cheer,
Creating magic, far and near.

Nature's Lullaby

The crickets chirp a nightly tune,
Underneath the watchful moon.
Stars twinkle in a cosmic choir,
As gentle breezes whisper higher.

The fountain gurgles a bubbly song,
While frogs join in, they can't go wrong.
A rhythm set by rustling leaves,
Nature's jesters, in playful heaves.

Fireflies glow like tiny lights,
Dancing around in silly flights.
Each little wink a joyful surprise,
As the night awakens laughter, not sighs.

Close your eyes, let the sounds flow,
Let the laughter and music grow.
In the arms of night, we gently sway,
An amusing lullaby, come what may.

The Essence of Eden

In a garden where giggles sprout,
Sunflowers smile, there's no doubt.
The tomatoes wear the sun's bright rays,
While zucchini jokes in leafy plays.

Thyme teases basil, it's quite the feat,
In a race to see who's the tastiest treat.
Carrots peek from the soil below,
With orange noses all in a row.

Cucumbers slip in a sly little skit,
While radishes blush, they can't take a hit.
The pumpkin strikes a pose so grand,
As vegetables frolic through the land.

In this Eden, laughter does bloom,
With each sprout, joy fills the room.
The essence of fun, both wild and free,
Nature's jesters, as bright as can be.

Symphony of Leaves

In the breeze, they dance a jig,
Minty youths and sage so big,
Parsley pranks and thyme's delight,
Cilantro hums beneath the light.

Basil's laughter fills the air,
As rosemary twirls without a care,
Oregano hops like a frog,
While tarragon sings to the log.

Scented Serenade

Dill's duet with garlic's glee,
Lemon balm winks at the bee,
Thyme plays soft on the lute,
While chives strut in a cute suit.

Mint brings giggles in its wake,
As lavender's jokes make us shake,
Cinnamon spins wildly around,
While a cumin comet's profound.

Garden of Echoes

In the garden, they chatter away,
Nasturtiums laugh all day,
Fennel tells tales of the sun,
While echinacea joins for fun!

Pitiful weeds sigh with envy,
As thyme's performance steals the frenzy,
A sagebrush slides and trips, oh dear,
Even nettles giggle, full of cheer.

Songs of the Soil

From the depths, a tune does arise,
Carrots hum in sweet surprise,
Potatoes dance with muddy toes,
While beets blush, hiding their woes.

The onions play a tearful tune,
As radishes rave by the moon,
Garlic leads a raucous ball,
And peas chuckle, standing tall.

Chants of the Flora

In the garden, plants do sing,
With leaves that sway and blossoms swing.
A dandelion does ballet moves,
While clovers join in silly grooves.

Mint whispers jokes in the cool breeze,
Sage cracks puns that make you wheeze.
Thyme's the master of disguise,
Pretending to be wise and spry!

Verdant Verses

Oregano rides a squirrel's back,
While parsley sketches in a track.
A rosemary crown on a ladybug,
Dances like it's on a tiny rug.

Basil tells tales of far-off lands,
Where dill is king, waving his hands.
Thyme brings laughter with cheeky grins,
Joining the fray as the fun begins!

The Elixir of Life

Lemon balm brews a fizzy charm,
While ginger roots dance with alarm.
A pot of tea starts a jam,
With raindrops tapping like a fam.

Fennel and sesame share a joke,
While lavender laughs as they poke.
Chamomile snoozes, snoring loud,
As sage brings laughter to the crowd.

Harmony Beneath the Canopy

Under the trees, the herbs conspire,
To start a band and raise the choir.
Cilantro plays the ukulele,
While chives go crazy, looking crazy!

A caper sings with a playful twirl,
As mugwort spins in a dizzy whirl.
In this grove, no frowns are seen,
Just giggles between the greenery keen!

Tales from the Thicket

In a forest where the daisies dance,
A squirrel slipped, lost his pants!
Chasing butterflies all day long,
He thought they'd join him for a song.

A rabbit tried to play the flute,
But ended up with carrot loot.
The music played, a bouncy beat,
And everyone was tapping feet.

The hedgehog wore a party hat,
Danced around with a whirling cat.
While mushrooms swayed in twirls and spins,
The laughter echoed, full of grins.

By sundown, all the critters cheered,
Forget the stew, no one had feared.
For in the thicket, jokes were keen,
And every leaf's a comedy scene.

Lush Lyrics

In the meadow of munchy greens,
A frog in tights sings off-key scenes.
He croaks a tune that makes kids giggle,
As ants below start to wiggle.

A parrot perched with bright blue wings,
Chimed in with absurd little things.
"Why did the berry blush so red?"
"Because it saw the salad spread!"

Petunias pranced with clumsy grace,
While daisies giggled, taking space.
With every breeze, there came a laugh,
As sunlight painted nature's staff.

At dusk, the crickets had their show,
Rubbing legs to make that glow.
In nature's choir, all bizarre,
They crooned beneath the evening star.

The Pulse of Petals

A sunflower tried to take a selfie,
But bees buzzed close, the focus was stealthy.
With petals fluffed, it posed quite proud,
While everyone laughed, a happy crowd.

The mint was minty, full of zest,
While thyme was just a bit depressed.
"I can't hang out; I'm a bit too thyme-y,"
Said carrot sticks, "Oh, just let's dine-y!"

Basil tried cooking up a scheme,
He wanted fame, a cooking dream.
But forgot the heat, oh what a plight,
His soup turned out all green and bright!

A parsley wink at its leafy kin,
"Let's cheer for each and every win!"
In the garden, laughter filled the air,
Where every plant had its own flair.

Melodic Whispers of the Woods

In the woods, the ferns like to chat,
As butterflies wear their vibrant hat.
A wise old owl spilled the tea,
"Did you hear the rumor about the bee?"

A porcupine with a prickly crown,
Told tales of clovers in the town.
"Don't ask the cat to lead the dance,
He steps on toes and takes a chance!"

The willows sighed, their leaves all sway,
While pebbles giggled in a playful way.
"Life's a trip, let's spread the cheer,
With each petite voice, the end is near!"

So join the band, don't be a bore,
The woods keep secrets, always more.
With jests and jives, they tell a tale,
Where every creature's joy prevails.

Green Reverie

In a garden quite absurd,
There's a pickle wearing a word.
It said, "Lettuce take a break!"
Then giggled like a cake.

Basil danced with spicy mint,
In a whirl like a pastel tint.
They twirled on the sunny patch,
Making all the flowers hatch.

A radish wore a silly hat,
While thyme played a game of cat.
They laughed as the wind would tease,
Oh, what fun to be with these!

But watch out! Here comes old sage,
In a robe, he took center stage.
With a wink and a twirl he spun,
Shouting, "Herbs are here for fun!"

The Language of Petals

A flower tried to speak one day,
But its words just flew away.
"I meant to say, 'Hello, good mate!'
Instead, I bloomed too late!"

Daisy asked the rose for clues,
On which color it should choose.
"I want to look bright and swell!"
Rose replied, "Just bloom and dwell!"

The orchids giggled in their rows,
As petals fluffed like velvet clothes.
"Do you think we've got the flair?"
Pansies said, "Oh, we're quite rare!"

Then came the bees with bandit glee,
Singing songs of mess and tea.
Amid the petals, laughter grew,
In conversations bright and new.

Aroma Among the Trees

Under a pine, a sprout did yawn,
"Evergreens just keep me drawn!"
It dreamed of scents from far away,
Of minty dreams and sage ballet.

Cinnamon bark made quite a show,
With nutmeg dancing to and fro.
They stirred up scents that filled the air,
And all the critters stopped to stare.

A ladybug with fancy stripes,
Joined in the fun, so free of types.
With wiggly legs it twirled around,
Creating laughter without a sound.

Then came the rain, with drops like cheer,
Moss joined in, whispering near.
Together they made such a scene,
With aromas ripe and fresh and green.

A Brew of Tranquility

In the kettle, chaos brews,
Leaves are swirling with no clues.
"Should we add some cinnamon?"
Ginger laughed and then he spun.

Chamomile played hide and seek,
While peppermint began to squeak.
"Hurry up, there's tea to sip!"
Said oolong with a playful flip.

Each ingredient had its say,
Mixing flavors in a fray.
"I'm too spicy!" said the thyme,
"Let's just chill with tea this time!"

Then they brewed a pot of joy,
A sipping game, no one's coy.
With laughter steaming on the rise,
Each sip unveiled their herb surprise.

Nature's Intonations

Nature sings a funny tune,
With leaves that dance around at noon.
The daisies giggle, the ferns just tease,
A band of greens that aim to please.

The trees are swaying, what a sight!
The bushes bounce with pure delight.
If plants could laugh, oh what a show,
Their jokes would sprout and surely grow!

The Saunter of Sage

Sage strutted by with a look so sly,
Trying to charm the thyme nearby.
"I've got wisdom," it said with glee,
"Join me for some tea, maybe three!"

The thyme rolled its eyes, took a leap,
"Not now, dear sage, I'm in too deep.
Busy with recipes, don't take too long,
But join me later, it won't be wrong!"

Kaleidoscope of Cultivation

In a garden of giggles, colors collide,
Mint makes a statement, it's got plenty of pride.
Basil's quite trendy with an air of chic,
While dill just winks—so quirky, so sleek!

Each plant a character, a vibrant part,
Creating a painting that pulls at the heart.
Together they flourish, a carnival scene,
In this playful patch, where all's evergreen!

Chords of the Clovers

Clovers croon with a twist of fate,
Four-leafed wonders that celebrate!
"Find me a luck," sang the green bunch,
While they shared giggles over a lunch.

The violets blushed, they heard their tune,
"This choir's delight, let's dance 'neath the moon!"
With every note, the harvest blooms,
A symphony sprouting in earthy rooms!

Orchard Overtures

In the orchard with peaches so ripe,
Squirrels dance, holding cups like a pipe.
Apples giggle, they're red and they're round,
While the oranges roll and tumble on ground.

Cherries chuckle with pits they can't hide,
Dancing all day, in their fruit-loving pride.
Lemons laugh loud, trying hard not to squawk,
As they play hopscotch on the warm garden block.

The bananas, they slip, but what a big show,
While the plums just sit, proving fruit can be slow.
In this orchard, joy is a fruit cocktail mix,
A giggly garden just bursting with tricks.

So come have a laugh where the fruit hangs so sweet,
In this joyous place, life is truly a treat!

Botanical Breath

In the garden of greens, the laughter erupts,
Where carrots tell jokes and herbs are corrupt.
Basil's a joker, with parsley in tow,
Snickering sweetly as they pull a fast show.

Thyme's got the rhythm, it sways to the score,
The rosemary croons, making herbs want more.
Mint joins the ruckus, a cheeky delight,
While dill goes on dancing into the night.

In this leafy cabaret, sage spills the tea,
As garlic stirs gossip and weaves a spree.
The garden's alive with a herbal café,
Where laughter and scents mingle and play.

Join the plant party, let's sip and we'll snack,
With giggles and scents, there's no looking back!

Melody of Mint

Minty fresh notes hum through the air,
As little green leaves dance without a care.
They twirl and they whirl, a whimsical sight,
Sipping on sunshine from morning to night.

Basil sings low, while cilantro plays high,
Chives laugh so hard, they sometimes just cry.
Pepper sneezes, and oh what a fuss,
While the garden erupts in a glorious rush!

Thyme plops a beat, and everyone grooves,
Dancing together, they're making their moves.
Each leaf has its part in this joyful ballet,
Creating a tune that's lively and gay.

So join in the fun, don't let it be missed,
In this fragrant concert, you simply can't resist!

Silent Symphony in the Garden

In the gentle garden where the shadows play,
Vegetables hush, ready for their sway.
Tomatoes whisper secrets, so ripe and so red,
While chard wraps up stories in green threads.

Radishes slyly giggle, all tucked underground,
Playing hide and seek without making a sound.
The beets wear their roots like a crown with a flair,
While melons daydream of parties up there.

Zucchini takes charge with a sly little grin,
As the pumpkins roll by, all ready to spin.
Insects play violins and bees hum along,
Creating a melody that's vibrant and strong.

So pull up a chair 'neath the leafy shade,
Join the quiet symphony the garden has made!

A Tune for the Thicket

In the thicket, critters dance,
Squirrels prance, giving herbs a glance.
A thyme sprig sings a silly song,
While the sage laughs, 'This won't take long.'

Rabbits hop with a giggling glee,
Chasing whiffs of parsley tea.
A rogue rosemary twirls, quite bold,
As the sun sets, their antics unfold.

Dancing daisies in the light,
Twist and turn till the moon is bright.
Every leaf a little joker,
Pulling pranks, they're quite the broker.

Bumblebees buzz with a cheeky cheer,
Spreading pollen, a nudge, then a leer.
Each herb, a jester, in nature's court,
In the thicket, join the raucous sport!

Lull of Lavender

Lavender dreams drift in the air,
With a wink, they tease and care.
'Count my flowers, just one more!'
And giggles erupt from the floral floor.

A bumblebee snores atop a bloom,
While daisies plot in a sunny room.
'Let's make a lemonade stand so sweet!'
'Till then, let's kick off our tiny feet!'

Petals flutter, a silly ballet,
Twisting and turning, come what may.
Each scent a chuckle, each swirl a cheer,
Even the moon stops by for a beer!

With a wink, the night bids adieu,
Lavenders chuckle, 'See you anew!'
Under the stars, their laughter flows,
In dreams of gardens, where joy always glows.

Fable of Foliage

In a forest where the ferns chatter,
Mysteries unfold with a twinkling clatter.
A tale of mint with a hidden stash,
Plotting pranks; oh, what a splash!

The elderberry, wise and spry,
Tells jokes that make the old oak sigh.
'Never trust a sprout with a grin!'
'Unless it's a beet; they're full of sin!'

From the willow, whispers rise high,
"Leaf me to my zany sky!"
While the flax giggles, dressing in blue,
As sunlight tickles the morning dew.

Oh, join the fables of foliage shrill,
With laughter echoing over the hill.
Wild tales spun by the green brigade,
A garden of jests that will never fade!

Poetic Petal Prose

Petals poof in a playful breeze,
Waltzing 'round with the greatest ease.
'Write a sonnet!' a daffodil dares,
While tulips gossip about their pairs.

In the meadow, butterflies flit,
Thinking of rhymes while they sit.
'Why did the bee buzz near the thyme?'
'It wanted a chat about the best rhyme!'

Petal prose on a paper boat,
Sailing along, never to gloat.
Each flower a writer, scribbling bright,
Their laughter echoing through the night.

So join the giggle, let your heart compose,
With whimsical verses the garden bestows.
In the world of petals, there's fun to expose,
Life is a poem, just follow your nose!

Fragrant Fusion

In a garden of smells, oh what a delight,
Basil and mint, they dance every night.
Thyme's on the beat, rosemary's cheer,
Parsley's got moves that bring us all near.

Chives are the backups, playing it cool,
While sage takes the lead, breaking all rules.
Oregano's spinning, garlic's off beat,
Together they shimmy, it's quite the sweet treat.

They giggle and wiggle, all dressed in green,
In this herbaceous world, nothing's routine.
With each twist and turn, they bring up a chuckle,
Who knew that a patch could lead to such buckle?

So grab your fresh herbs, and join in the fun,
Transforming our meals, one dance at a run.
Life in the kitchen, a jolly old show,
With each splash of flavor, the laughter will grow.

The Herbal Chorus

Gathered together, they form quite the band,
With marjoram's rhythm and cilantro's hand.
Dill's got a tune, it tickles the ear,
While chervil brings sweetness, oh what a cheer!

In pots with a purpose, they sing every day,
Dropping their notes, as they sway and play.
Mint leads the charge, a fresh little sprite,
While tarragon's charm twirls into the night.

A symphony brewed in a cauldron below,
With simmering laughs, as the aromas grow.
They harmonize boldly, a flavorful show,
Making a dish that sings, oh so low!

So join in the revel, let your spirits rise,
With herbs on the stage, there's no need for disguise.
Each pinch and each dash, a note in the ear,
Let's feast with a tune, and give a good cheer!

Ode to the Wilds

In fields of green, a riotous dance,
Dandelions giggle, given a chance.
Nettles invite you, with pokes and pricks,
But wait—don't be fooled—it's their clever tricks!

Clover's a jester, throwing its hats,
While wild garlic whispers, "Come join the chat."
With violets blooming, sweet stories unfold,
Each petal a giggle, a secret retold.

Thickets of thyme play peek-a-boo games,
As buttercups wink, yelling, "Look at our aims!"
The earthy ol' sage, wise enough to know,
Joy's found in the wild when we let laughter flow.

So here we shall revel, amidst sun and shade,
With nature's own cast, and smiles that won't fade.
Each wild bloom a punchline, each leaf like a rhyme,
Witness the comedy, energized with time.

Blooms and Breezes

Petals flutter by, with a ticklish grace,
Breezes approach in a dash, just in case.
Zinnias laugh loud, as the wind gives a spin,
While lavenders sigh, with a soft, fragrant grin.

Boys and girls twirl through the bright sunny days,
Sniffing the blossoms in whimsical ways.
Chasing each flower, oh what a delight,
As bees buzz along, having quite the night.

The sun's a good buddy, laughing above,
While clovers and daisies show off their love.
In this flowery realm, we dance with the breeze,
With blossoms as friends, life's humor's a tease.

So let's cultivate joy and giggles galore,
With a bouquet of smiles, we couldn't want more.
In gardens of whimsy, we find our sweet thrill,
With blooms and with breezes, our spirits they fill.

Rhythms of the Earth

In gardens green, where laughter grows,
Bees dance around in silly rows.
With flowers winking, colors bright,
They tickle our noses with pure delight.

A daisy sneezes, pollen bursts,
While pansies giggle, quenching their thirst.
Earth wears a crown of scents and glee,
As worms do the cha-cha, oh what a spree!

The sun spills juice in cheerful streams,
While veggies plot their giggly schemes.
Tomatoes blush in the buzzing crowd,
And carrots dance, all silly and proud.

Let's toast to dirt, and mud pies divine,
With whipped cream clouds and sunshine wine.
The rhythms urge us, nature's cheer,
Embrace the playful, bring it near!

Alchemy of Aromas

In the pot, herbs jive and laugh,
Mint tells stories—what a chaff!
Basil winks from the savory side,
While thyme does cartwheels, full of pride.

A sprinkle of joy, a dash of cheer,
Lemongrass plays hide-and-seek near.
Cilantro smirks, oh what a tease,
As garlic waltzes with the breeze.

From kitchen chaos, a feast will rise,
With spice-filled hugs and flavor surprise.
Cooks join hands in a vibrant fling,
Chopping and stirring, oh let it sing!

But watch your toes as the peppers sway,
For chili jigs, wanting to play.
In this cauldron, laughter is the key,
A recipe of fun, just let it be!

Melody in the Meadow

In fields where daisies strum their strings,
Butterflies flutter and tune their wings.
Crickets play the nighttime song,
While the moon hums along all night long.

The grass gets tickled by a gentle breeze,
As daisies spin and swirl with ease.
They sing of springs with a laugh so sweet,
While earthworms tap dance beneath our feet.

A gopher's hiccup, a squirrel's cheer,
Nature's concert, we gather near.
With hummingbirds flapping in jazzy flight,
It's a meadow party, full of delight!

So grab your friends and dance along,
With earthy beats, we can't go wrong.
In nature's band, we're all a part,
Each note a beat of a joyful heart!

Petals in the Breeze

Petals pirouette on a summer's day,
Twirling around in a silly ballet.
With butterflies donning their fanciest dress,
They giggle and glide, oh what a mess!

The poppies chuckle, the roses snicker,
As pollen hitchhikes, playing the trickster.
"Who needs a kite?" the daisies decree,
"We'll float on the wind, just wait and see!"

A ladybug jives, twerking so fine,
While sunflowers rock, sipping on sunshine.
"Let's sway to the rhythm of nature's breeze,
With laughter and cheer, we'll dance with ease!"

So join the petals, lift your heart's song,
In this floral circus, you can't go wrong.
On breezy adventures, let joy be your guide,
As petals and laughter collide!

Chorus of the Wildflowers

In a meadow, blooms bright and bold,
Where daisies gossip, stories unfold.
Sunflowers dance, with their heads held high,
As poppies giggle and butterflies fly.

The violets wear hats, oh what a sight,
While clovers play tag in morning light.
Dandelions poof with a sneezy flair,
They spread their wishes, a breeze in the air.

With petals that shade, the gossip's so grand,
Chatter of bees, as they buzz and band.
The daisies nod, "Let's throw a bash!"
But the lilies just sigh, "Oh, it's bound to clash!"

Yet in this patch, all frolic and sing,
The laughter of flora is the wild's bling.
So join in the fun, lose all that stress,
In this flower frolic, everyone's blessed!

The Language of Thorns

Among the brambles, a prickly jest,
A rose bud winks, it's feeling its best.
Thorns whisper secrets as the night unfolds,
'Beware of the rabbits,' it coyly scolds.

The thistles chuckle in a spiky cheer,
With a throny grin, they call for a beer.
Mr. Cactus, oh, he's quite the tease,
In a desert party, he's hard to please!

A snarky old ivy grumbles away,
"Get off my leaves, that's too much in play!"
The holly sprigs hook and laugh with glee,
"No offense intended, just a holiday spree!"

So raise a toast to the thorns and their tales,
In the realm of spiky, laughter prevails.
A banquet of jokes under moonlit skies,
Where thorns are the jesters, oh what a surprise!

Echoes from the Apothecary

In the tower of potions, the bottles chime,
A walking herb sings in perfect rhyme.
"Ginger's too spicy, please douse his flames!"
While chamomile giggles at all of their games.

Rosemary's cooking up tales for a feast,
While peppermint teases, "I'm more than a beast!"
Basil is plotting a culinary trick,
"Add just a pinch, or you'll ruin it quick!"

The sage in the corner, wise beyond years,
Whispers to all, "Release all your fears."
But thyme rolls its eyes, "Let's get to the tea!"
And laughter erupts; it's a party, whee!

So potions bubble and laughter flows,
In this herbal circus, anything goes.
With a sprinkle of laughter and a dash of glee,
The echoes of herbs are wild and free!

Vibrant Whispers

In gardens where colors dance, oh what fun,
Petunias gossip under the sun.
"Are you pink? Are you blue? What's your hue?"
"Just call me fabulous," one flower flew.

Marigolds chime with a bright hello,
As daisies join in for the grand show.
Lavender hums a sweet serenade,
While the poppies sway, in a vibrant parade.

Geraniums boast of their fragrance so neat,
While ferns look askance, "You think you're elite?"
"Oh, I'm just leafy and rather aloof,"
Says a shy little sprout not wanting to scoof.

So sing with the blossoms, in chaos and cheer,
As nature's wild laughter draws everyone near.
In whispers of colors, we find our tune,
And dance in the garden, beneath the bright moon!

Nectar in the Nook

In the nook where bees do buzz,
A flower sings and gives us fuzz.
The ants march in with tiny hats,
While ladybugs are chatting chitchats.

Mint leaves dance a silly jig,
Thyme's got moves that are really big.
The sage tells jokes, a bit offbeat,
While lavender brings snacks to eat.

The sun sets low, a twilight scene,
As rosemary wears a leafy green.
With each sip of tea, we laugh and cheer,
The plants unite, it's party here!

So here's to greens that make us smile,
With quirky leaves and quirky style.
In every pot, a tale unfolds,
Nature's fun, it never gets old.

Cadence of Clovers

Clover patches, four leaf finds,
Dancing in winds, playful minds.
Grasshoppers play the ukulele,
While dandelions cheer, oh so gaily.

Each petal's wink, a secret told,
With bumbles buzzing, joy unfold.
A picnic planned with all things green,
We laugh 'til we're a silly scene.

The sprigs of thyme join in a tune,
While chives dance 'neath the silver moon.
With every nibble, we burst with glee,
Nature's buffet, come taste with me!

So raise a glass of herbal dew,
To clovers dancing, just for you.
A merry jig in emerald shade,
The joy of plants shall never fade.

Harmonizing with Heritage

Grandma's garden, full of joy,
With scents that tease, a clever ploy.
Oregano's got a sassy shout,
    As basil prances all about.

Herbs in rows, a lively debate,
Thyme claims it's the true soulmate.
While parsley snickers, "I'm the star!"
Together they make a bizarre bazaar.

The garlic bulb takes center stage,
With stories of old, it sets the age.
Each sprout a compadre, bold and loud,
They laugh so hard they draw a crowd.

So join the fun, where flavors mix,
With quirky herbs and herbal tricks.
In every pot, a family tale,
    Get ready for a fragrant gale!

The Symphony of the Seasons

Spring whispers sweet in blooming scents,
As parsley dances, no pretense.
Summer sings with scents so bold,
Garlic chives prance, no need to scold.

Autumn croaks, with leaves so bright,
Cilantro winks in fading light.
Winter's frost brings a chilly cheer,
Yet mint remains, always near.

In this mix of spicy laughs,
Nature's gifts provide fine crafts.
Each season brings a brand-new song,
Herbs and laughter, where we all belong.

So gather round for a verdant fest,
With pots of green, they are the best.
Nature's tunes create the charm,
In the garden, we find our calm.

Soft Notes on the Wind

In the garden, herbs do dance,
Mint and thyme take a chance.
A chive tickles a buzzing bee,
Sage whispers secrets, oh so free.

Lemon balm laughs in the sun,
Giggling petals, oh what fun!
Basil twirls, what a sight,
With the parsley, they unite.

Nature's Castanets

Oregano claps with glee,
While rosemary shakes, can you see?
A cacophony of scents and sights,
Making music through day and night.

Garlic strings up a groovy beat,
Cilantro joins, what a treat!
Chili peppers add some spice,
Together they roll, oh so nice!

Tune of the Tendrils

Tendrils curl and vine around,
Playing notes from the ground.
Kale struts in leafy green,
While broccoli dons a crown, a queen!

Radishes drum with their roots,
Potatoes join in with their hoots.
A trumpet from the turnip's head,
Chiming laughter, where they tread.

The Symphony of Growth

In the patch, a leafy band,
Cabbages sway, so well-planned.
Spinach sings in a low hum,
While carrots tap, oh so dumb!

Chives create a ticklish score,
While pumpkins roll and roar.
With every sprout and every seed,
A leafy tune, indeed, indeed!

Cacophony of Citrus

In the orchard where lemons rant,
Limes gossip with a jaunty chant.
Oranges roll in a citrus race,
Grapefruits frown, they just can't relate.

The tangerines tease, they wiggle and dance,
Squeezing each joke like it's their chance.
A zesty crew, they all take a bow,
The jester in green, a lime, takes a vow.

Peelings laugh as they tumble and twirl,
Dancing amidst their zesty swirl.
With every squeeze, the punchlines fly,
This fruity feud will never die.

In this cacophony, a sweet delight,
Fruit jokes heard until the night.
So grab a glass for a punchy cheer,
Citrus shenanigans, let's raise a beer!

The Breeze's Ballad

On windy days, the mint leaves sway,
Tickling the taste buds that come out to play.
Basil sings from the window sill,
A light-hearted breeze, a fragrant thrill.

The chives join in with a raucous glee,
Playing tag with the rosemary tree.
Onions laugh, but they can't stay bright,
In the game of scents, they fade from sight.

Meanwhile, the parsley prances around,
"Sniff me, sniff me!" is the game that they found.
The sage mumbles stories of times gone by,
With thyme as the DJ spinning tunes high.

A ballad of laughter fills the warm air,
Herbs in a dance, without a care.
As the breeze rustles leaves to the beat,
Nature's fun concert, oh what a treat!

Enchanted Essence

In a garden of dreams, the petals giggle,
With a wink from the flowers, they start to wiggle.
Lavender whispers sweet nothings in pink,
While dandelions puff out, "What do you think?"

The petals debate, "Who's the prettiest here?"
Roses declare, "It's definitely clear!"
But violets jump in with a shout,
"Without me, your prattle's all just a spout!"

The scent of jasmine sneaks in the fray,
With elderflower saying, "I like it my way!"
As bees buzz around, their wings in a trance,
It's a flowery party, everyone's in a dance.

So here in the garden, where chaos reigns,
Essence of laughter spills like the rains.
With every blossom, there's joy to amend,
In this enchanted plot, the fun will not end!

Tails of Thyme

Once upon a thyme, a joke was told,
About a wise herb, so cunning and bold.
With a twist of the stalk and a hop so spry,
Thyme wiggled its leaves, waving hi-hi-hi!

Basil chuckled, "You're so very punny!"
While dill rolled its eyes, all bright and sunny.
But when parsley piped up with a rhyme.
"I'm garnish-ing laughs, it's all in good time!"

In the patch of mirth, all herbs come alive,
With stories of roots and how they survive.
The fennel tells tales of flavor and zest,
While marjoram dreams of spice at its best.

So gather 'round now, let thyme take a stand,
In this leafy laughter, all carefully planned.
With each little herb, a chuckle and smile,
These tails of thyme are always worth while!

Tonic for the Soul

A minty breeze, a joyful twist,
Ginger leaps with a spicy fist.
Lemon balm laughing, so fresh and bright,
Chasing away the worries at night.

Thyme's witty punchlines in tea,
Dancing in cups, oh so carefree.
A pinch of humor, a dash of cheer,
Sipping the giggles, let out a cheer!

Rosemary reminds us, don't be so serious,
With laughter and warmth, we are delirious.
Parsley whispers jokes in your ear,
A roast and a toasting, my dear, oh dear!

With every sip and every jest,
Nature's gifts are truly the best.
So raise your cup to the funny and bold,
A tonic for the heart, stories told!

Notes of Nature's Chorus

In the garden, a melody plays,
Basil sings sweet in hilarious ways.
Cilantro's tickle, it's hard to resist,
Dancing with lavender, oh what a twist!

Chives are giggling, long and green,
Their jokes are as fresh as they are keen.
Oregano winks with a spicy remark,
An orchestra thriving, lighting the spark!

Thyme strumming soft, with rosemary's strife,
Singing about the joys of plant life.
Every leaf tells a story so grand,
Nature's own band, oh isn't it grand?

So come take a seat, don't be shy,
Let the notes of green pass you by.
In the chorus of laughter, let go of the fuss,
For in this lively garden, we all can trust!

Serenade of Sage and Thyme

Oh sage, with wisdom and tips to impart,
Whispers of secrets that tickle the heart.
Thyme takes the stage with its cheeky appeal,
A duet of banter, a savory reel!

Lavish laughter in every pot,
A bubbling brew, oh what a plot!
Mix in some humor, a salt of surprise,
Each sip brings a grin, a feast for the eyes.

Dill joins the fun, with punchlines so spry,
Telling sweet tales as the moments fly by.
Basil chuckles, "Just have a bite!"
Every herb is giggling, what pure delight!

So raise your glass to this herbal band,
Dancing together, much more than a fad.
In the symphony of spices, we find our tune,
With sage and thyme, life's a merry cartoon!

Lullabies of Lavender

Under the stars, where lavender dreams,
Whispers of comfort burst at the seams.
A sleepy smile, the night wraps around,
In fields of soft purple, joy is profound.

The breeze carries stories, sweet and absurd,
With chamomile's help, you'll never feel curbed.
Echoes of giggles drift through the air,
Swaying in slumber, without a care.

Valerian sings softly, enchanting your night,
With friendly banter 'til morning's first light.
A lullaby woven with humor and grace,
In dreamland, the herbs take their place.

So nestle down close, let the laughter unfurl,
In the land of the herbs, where fun is the pearl.
With every sweet whisper, feel worries dissolve,
In soothing embrace, let your heart evolve!

Chimeras of Chamomile

In a garden where teasies play,
Chamomile dreams the night away.
With fussy bees that dance and twirl,
And sleepy mice in a cotton swirl.

They sip on nectar, feeling grand,
Plotting pranks across the land.
A chamomile hat, oh what a sight,
A drowsy mouse, ready for flight!

The daisies giggle, the roses gasp,
At herbal tales that make them clasp.
They've brewed a potion with a twist,
To make the sunflowers do a little twist!

So up in the air, they float with glee,
What fun it is, this herbal spree!
A chamomile song, a magical rhyme,
In this silly garden, life is sublime!

Sweet Songs of Sweetgrass

In fields where sweetgrass sways in tune,
Frogs croak under the smiling moon.
They sing of croquettes with a sassy flair,
While grasshoppers hop without a care.

With crunchy munchies and wild tea spills,
They throw herb parties with zest and thrills.
An owl named Phil does the waltz so sly,
While fragrant breezes on by gently sigh.

A catnip chorus joins the show,
Calling all critters, come see the flow!
As sweetgrass jokes make everyone laugh,
They dance to the rhythm, oh what a craft!

So, raise your glasses of minty delight,
To sweetgrass songs that entice the night!
With whispers of echo from tree to crescent,
Even the crickets join in, so pleasant!

Piquant Poetry

A basil leaf whispers a story so bold,
Of garlic's antics, both spicy and old.
With cilantro's giggles and thyme's wise grin,
Their piquant tales are where fun begins!

In the pot, they simmer with laughter and fright,
Zesty debates on who's the best bite.
Oregano argues with chili so hot,
While slips of pepper laugh in the pot.

Tomatoes join in, all saucy and red,
Creating a sonnet from things they've said.
In this kitchen, it's more than just stew,
It's a flavorful chorus, a rave for the crew!

They dance on the table in a comedy act,
With flavors united, a savory pact.
So grab a fork, join the feast with a cheer,
For piquant poetry is best shared here!

Rhymes of Resilience

Through storms and sun, the herbs do sway,
With laughter brightening up each day.
Mint shares tales of zest-filled fights,
While rosemary shines with all of its lights.

Sage looks wise, with a smirk so sly,
While tarragon dreams of reaching the sky.
They bounce back easy, like spring's first bloom,
With nature embracing them in fragrant room.

Lemons chuckle as they take a flip,
Ginger canter, oh what a trip!
In the face of ruin, herbs find their way,
Creating a laughter that brightens the gray.

So here's to resilience, a garden grown,
In every herb, a funny bone!
With giggles and grins, they plant their seeds,
In herbal adventures, they meet their needs!

Echoes of Eucalyptus

In a forest where koalas play,
Eucalyptus leaves steal the day.
They dance and twirl in the breeze,
Giggles float like buzzing bees.

The branches twist, a wild ballet,
While critters munch in a leafy buffet.
With every crunch, a giggle grows,
Nature's laughter in the flows.

Silly squirrels join the fun,
Flipping leaves under the sun.
With each gust, the laughter swells,
Echoes of joy through leafy dwell.

Oh, the pranks that trees can pull,
Shaking branches, it's quite the cull!
As eucalyptus leaves take flight,
Nature's chuckles in pure delight.

The Sway of Soft Herbs

In the garden, herbs sway and sing,
Basil twirls like it's the spring king.
Mint does a jig, just look at it prance,
Cilantro joins in; it's a spicy romance!

Thyme's in a hurry, can't find the beat,
Parsley laughing, tapping its feet.
Oregano rolls in, full of sass,
Dancing around like it's first in class!

Chives are giggling, waving around,
While rosemary grins, calm and profound.
It's not just herbs; it's a party parade,
With each sprig a role, expertly played!

Under the sun, they spin, they sway,
Creating joy in a leafy ballet.
Catch their moves, as they frolic and play,
Life's best moments—herbs lead the way!

Vibrations of the Vines

In the vineyard, the grapes have a rhyme,
Bopping and swaying, it's party time!
With leaves as their skirts, they whirl and twine,
Every cluster bursting with fun divine.

A cheeky chardonnay whispers sweet,
While merlot stomps with two large feet.
Each twist and turn's a reason to cheer,
Laughter bubbles up like some fine, fizzy beer!

The vines all chatter, having a ball,
Dancing together, great fun for all.
With a bounce, they shimmy, in sunlight they bask,
Who knew grapes could be such a lively task?

From sunrise to sunset, they sway in delight,
Sipping on sunshine, oh what a sight!
In the vineyard, joy and laughter are fine,
Listen close, feel the vibrations of the vine!

Swaying in Serenity

In fields of green where daisies lie,
Herbs take a breath, beneath the sky.
Lavender giggles with a soothing sigh,
While sage rolls over, too tired to try.

Charming chamomile, in sweet repose,
Tickles the petals, as soft wind blows.
Nature's lullabyes put worries to sleep,
As herbs sway gently, their secrets they keep.

Lemon balm chuckles, as breezes toast,
In this peaceful dance, they love the most.
With every sway and subtle sway,
Even the crickets join in the play!

The sun sets low, wrapping the day,
Where herbs find joy as they softly sway.
In this dance of green, hearts are so free,
Embracing tranquility with glee!

The Color of Calm

In the garden, colors play,
Green and brown, a lively sway.
Plants wear hats made of leafy lace,
Making sunflowers giggle in their place.

Mint winks while the basil sways,
Sage tells jokes on lazy days.
Thyme shares secrets with the breeze,
Laughing softly, oh what a tease!

Carrots dance in their cozy beds,
"Guess our color?" they playfully said.
Radishes blush in rosy glow,
Always ready for a garden show.

Roses giggle, petals twirl,
While beans do the twist and whirl.
In this patch where laughter grows,
A bouquet of joy, everyone knows.

Harmonies from Harvest

Gather 'round for the harvest feast,
Pickled radish, oh what a beast!
Lettuce whispers with a crunchy cheer,
"Too much dressing? Never fear!"

Tomatoes joke with a little zest,
"I'm ripened and ready, I'm the best!"
Peppers are spicy, vibrant and bright,
"Chili dance-off?" What a delight!

Onions peel back layers of fun,
Making the chef wipe tears, then run!
Garlic's breath? A pungent affair,
Still, it charms every cook with flair.

Pumpkins roll with a hearty laugh,
All dressed up for autumn's path.
With each bite, giggles we share,
A feast of joy beyond compare!

Cures in the Canopy

Up in the trees, whispers we find,
The laughter of leaves, sweet and kind.
Eucalyptus shares minty delights,
While tarragon twirls on starry nights.

Aloe's got gel for summer skin,
"Apply with love, let the laughs begin!"
Lavender's scent floats through the air,
"Calm down, buddy, no need to glare!"

Ginger's got spunk, it's known far and wide,
"Kick of the spice? Come take a ride!"
Chamomile's tea, a warm cozy hug,
"Pour me a cup, let's dance like a bug!"

In the canopy, where joy is grown,
Nature's pharmacy, laughter is sown.
Each herb a friend, in colors so bright,
Cures mixed with chuckles, pure delight!

Soft Symphony of Soil

Softly beneath, the soil sings low,
"Plant your worries, watch them grow!"
Earthworms wiggle with mischievous cheer,
"Turn my tunes up, lend me your ear!"

Grains of sand whisper sweetly,
"Who knew we could be so cheeky?"
Peat parties, where moss does sway,
"Turf us into spring, come what may!"

Garden gnomes with their tiny hats,
Guarding secrets, laughing with cats.
"Don't step here, or you'll disrupt the beat!"
In the soft soil, joy's complete!

Roots intertwine in a playful dance,
"Life's too short; give joy a chance!"
With each plant poking toward the sun,
The symphony plays, and laughter won!

Breath of the Botanicals

In the garden, potions brew,
Chasing dreams that smell like dew.
Minty laughter fills the air,
Basil winks without a care.

Thyme tickles the morning sun,
While sleepy parsley tries to run.
Oregano starts a dance so wild,
Dill just giggles, sweet and mild.

Sage is wise, insists he's cool,
Yet he trips, now who's the fool?
Rosemary joins, a spicy tease,
They tumble down like autumn leaves.

From this plot of leafy glee,
Blissfully strange, so bonkers free.
With every sip, a chuckle blooms,
In the land where plant life zooms.

Song of the Sunrise Herbs

Morning calls, the herbs awake,
With every shake, a slight earthquake.
Chives are giggling, doing flips,
While cilantro struts, showing hips.

Buds parade with sunny cheer,
Parsley jokes, "I'm the one to steer!"
Lavender hums a sleepy tune,
While thyme dodges the afternoon.

Just when basil tries a spin,
A gust of wind sends him in!
He twirls around to land with grace,
Sage won't stop, he's in the race.

With every herb, a silly tale,
Laughter echoes through the vale.
Sunrise herbs, a joyful sight,
In our garden, pure delight.

Whispers of Green

In the shade, a thyme so bold,
Whispers secrets, never told.
Chives giggle, "Guess my height?"
"Twice as tall as yours," they bite.

Mint makes mischief, oh so sly,
"Where'd my leaf go? It took to fly!"
Dill rolls down a sunny slope,
Spins and grins, a jar of hope.

The sage, a storyteller grand,
Tales of herbs across the land.
Cilantro chimed in with a laugh,
"Best with tacos, not just half!"

Under leaves of vibrant sheen,
We dance, rejoice in what's unseen.
Nature's wild and funny show,
In our hearts, this joy will grow.

Nature's Melodies

Amidst the greens, what joy does show,
Herbs in band, ready to go.
Basil strums on leafy strings,
While chamomile softly sings.

On a twig, a funky beat,
Minty notes, oh what a treat!
Thyme claps hands and stomps along,
Each leaf whispers a silly song.

Oregano leads a merry dance,
With rosemary in a twirl of chance.
The garden grooves beneath the sun,
Laughing herbs, a race for fun.

So join the tune and sway so free,
Where plants and laughter dance with glee.
Nature's music, vibrant and bright,
From our leafy friends, pure delight!

The Art of Growing Stillness

In a garden full of quiet,
The weeds play hide and seek,
The herbs giggle in their greens,
While the carrots just look sleek.

A snail took a stroll, so slow,
Whispering tales of tea,
For a leaf is just a leaf, you know,
Unless it's steeped with glee!

The basil tells the sage a joke,
But the thyme just rolls its eyes,
With every joke, it's no hoax,
The basil's humor flies!

So let's cultivate this laughter,
In the dirt, let joy abound,
As the rain comes, we'll cheer after,
Nature's giggles all around!

Chants of Chia and Chamomile

Chia seeds dance, oh what a sight,
In puddles of pudding, they delight,
Chamomile sits, so calm and sweet,
Dreaming of honey that can't be beat.

They sing to the bees, a wobbly tune,
With petals drenched in afternoon,
Chamomile whispers, 'Let's take a break,'
While Chia shouts, 'For goodness' sake!'

In cozy corners of a teacup world,
Laughter blooms as aromas swirl,
A sip of sunshine, a nibble of glee,
With every brew, we're wild and free!

Together they swirl, a wholesome spell,
Transforming troubles into a swell,
For every drop is a gut-filled cheer,
Chants of chia—oh, how we hear!

Lyrical Leaves of Life

Leaves fluttering down, a chorus of green,
In this leafy ballet, everything's seen,
Oregano twirls in a spicy jive,
While cilantro mocks, 'Can't you see I thrive?'

Thick rosemary struts with a sturdy grace,
While parsley gets lost in a leafy race,
'Come catch me,' it laughs, 'I'm the spice of life!'
As the others just chuckle, free from strife.

A minty melody cuts through the air,
With whispers of warmth, a soothing affair,
'Halt, take a breath,' says the sage so wise,
'In the rhythm of flavor, joy never dies!'

So dance in the garden, let laughter unfold,
In the song of the leaves, great stories are told,
A festival of flavors awaits when we play,
In the lyrical leaves, forever we'll sway!

Tapestry of Verdant Vibes

We weave a tapestry, bright and bold,
With nettles and laughter—pure gold,
Cabbage rolls in, wearing a grin,
While mint claims, 'I'm the freshest kin!'

Through the petals and stems, we play our part,
Building a garden straight from the heart,
Green beans giggle as they sway to the beat,
While radishes dance, oh what a treat!

Come join the fun, don't be shy,
In this patch of joy, we'll reach for the sky,
Parsley can pirouette, thyme can spin,
Together united, they all dive in!

So sow seeds of laughter, let them grow tall,
In this verdant joy, there's enough for all,
Harvest the smiles, the giggles, the vibes,
In our patch of green, where nature imbibes.

www.ingramcontent.com/pod-product-compliance
Lightning Source LLC
Chambersburg PA
CBHW051636160426
43209CB00004B/678